MY FIRST BOO

COLOR BY NUMBERS

Woo! jr
kids activities

Copyright © 2021 Woo! Jr. Kids Activities LLC / Wendy Piersall. All rights reserved.

Woo! Jr. Kids Activities Founder: Wendy Piersall

Book Layout by: Michael Koch, Lilia Garvin, Ethan Piersall

Published by DragonFruit, an imprint of Mango Publishing, a division of Mango Publishing Group, Inc.

For permission requests, please contact the publisher at:

Mango Publishing Group
2850 Douglas Road, 2nd Floor
Coral Gables, FL 33134 USA
info@mango.bz

For special orders, quantity sales, course adoptions and corporate sales, please email the publisher at sales@mango.bz. For trade and wholesale sales, please contact Ingram Publisher Services at customer.service@ingramcontent.com or +1.800.509.4887.

My First Book of Color by Numbers

ISBN: 978-1-64250-715-7

BISAC: JNF001010, JUVENILE NONFICTION / Activity Books / Coloring

My First Color by Numbers Book

Time to solve puzzles by coloring! Each picture in this book needs 1-10 colors, and you use those colors to finish the drawing.

In the "Stained Glass" puzzle on the right, you would color 1 with purple, 2 with blue, 3 with green, and 4 with pink. Each puzzle is different, so check the colors used on each page!

Can you color the bird?

1 Blue **2** Yellow

Stained Glass

Fill in the colors!

1 **Purple**   2 **Blue**   3 **Green**   4 **Pink**

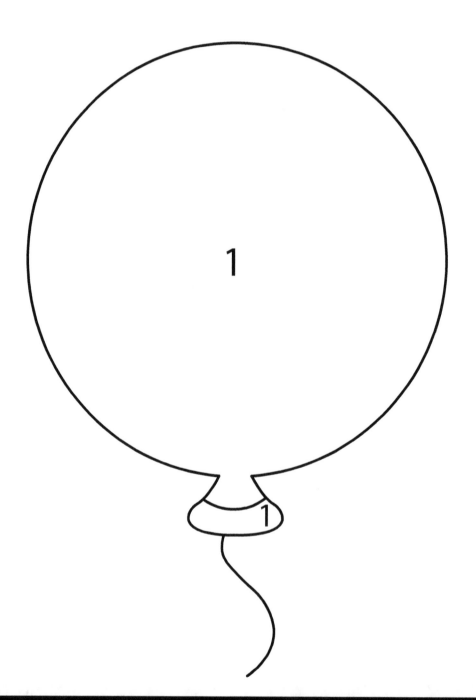

1 Red

Shooting Star

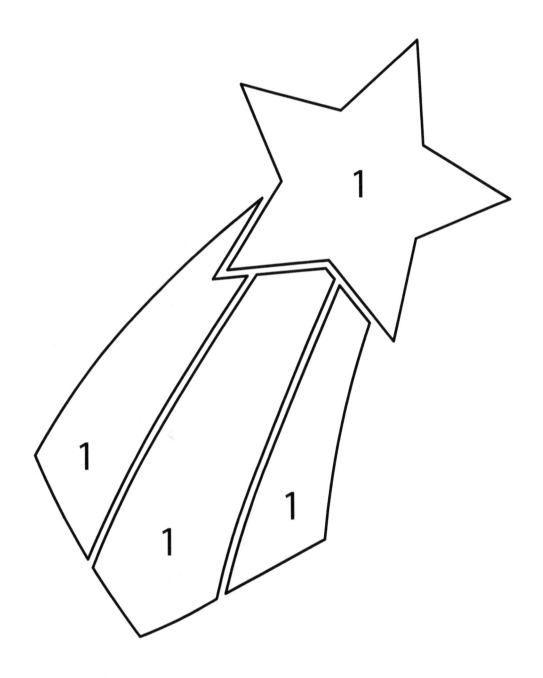

1 Yellow

Empty Envelope

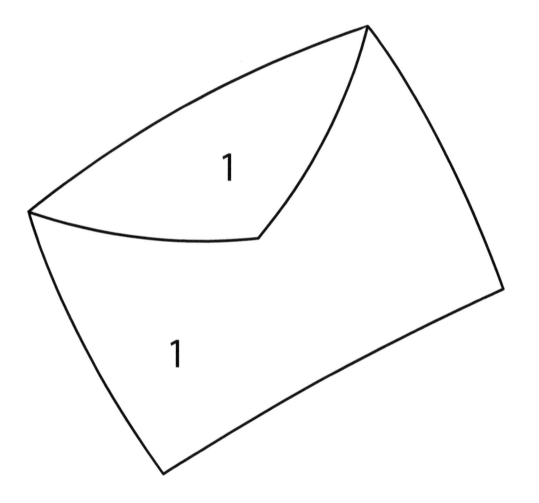

1 Yellow

Bubbly Beaker

1 Sky Blue **2** White

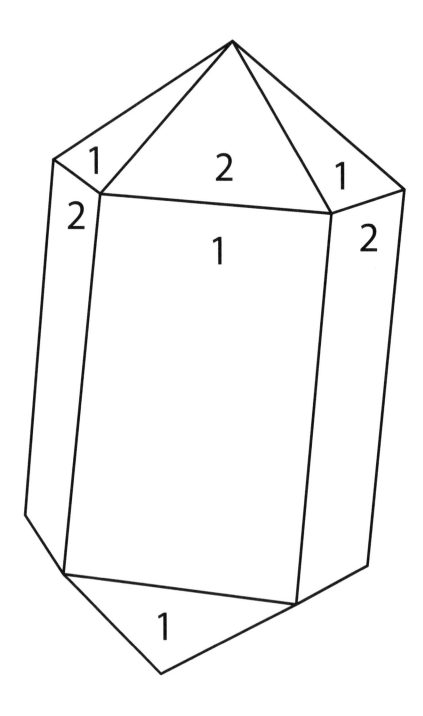

1 Magenta   2 Pink

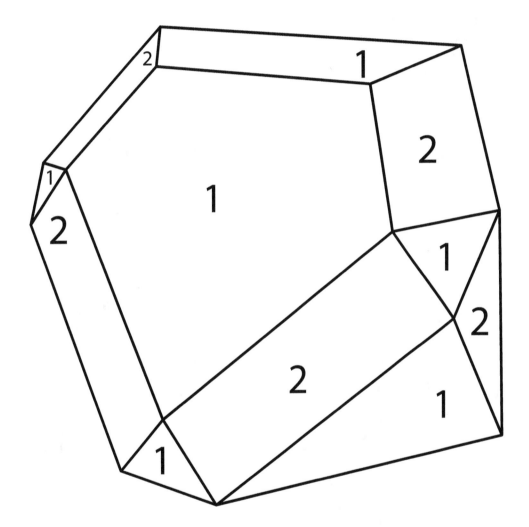

Fancy Phone

1 Red **2** Black

Practical Pen

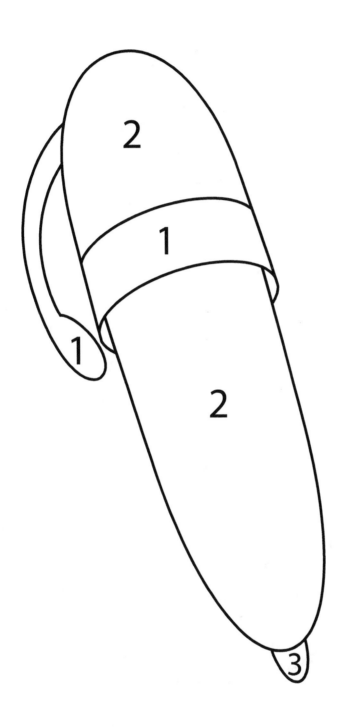

Pretty Party Hat

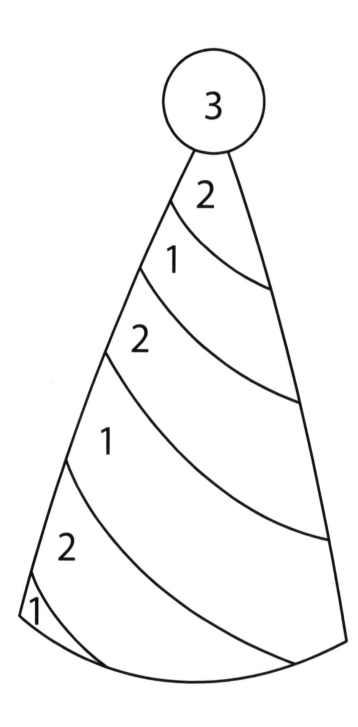

Brainy Book

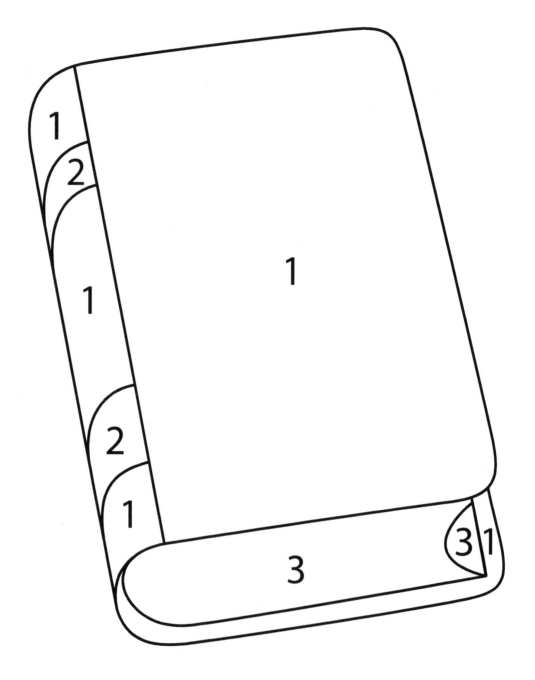

1 Brown 2 Tan 3 White

Bulky Backpack

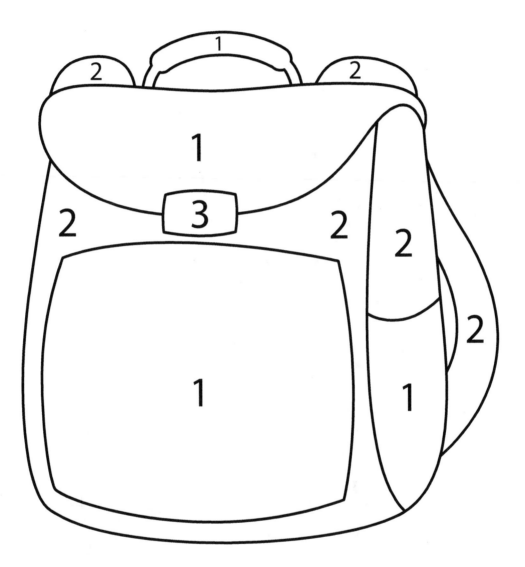

Magnificent Medal

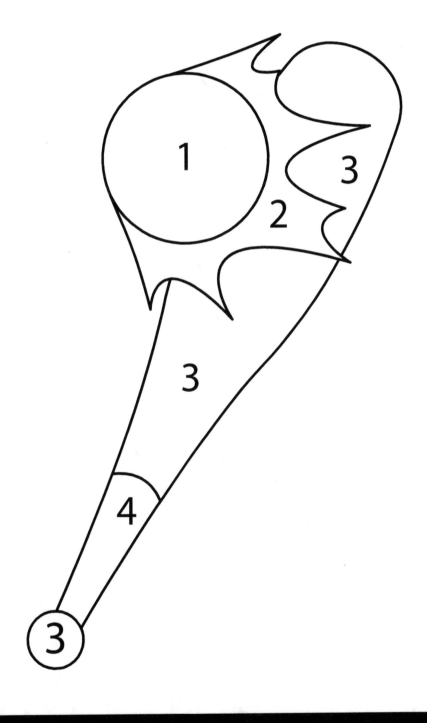

1 White 2 Orange 3 Brown 4 Black

Terrific Tennis

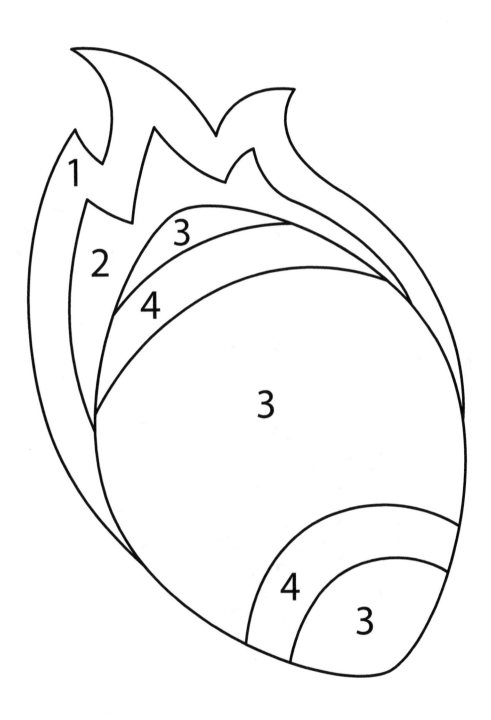

1 Orange   2 Red   3 Brown   4 White

Bouncy Basketball

Proper Pencil

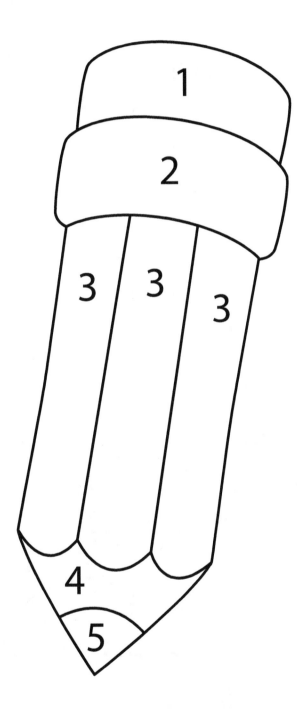

Grand Globe

cute Cat

Clicky Camera

cold cone

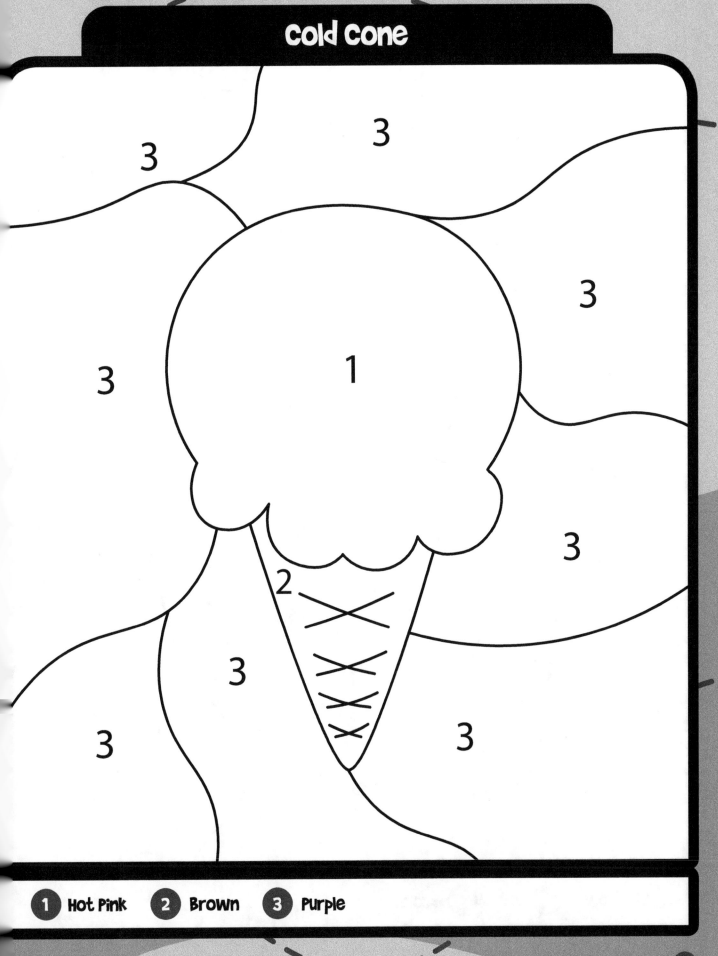

1 Hot Pink 2 Brown 3 Purple

Fun Fries

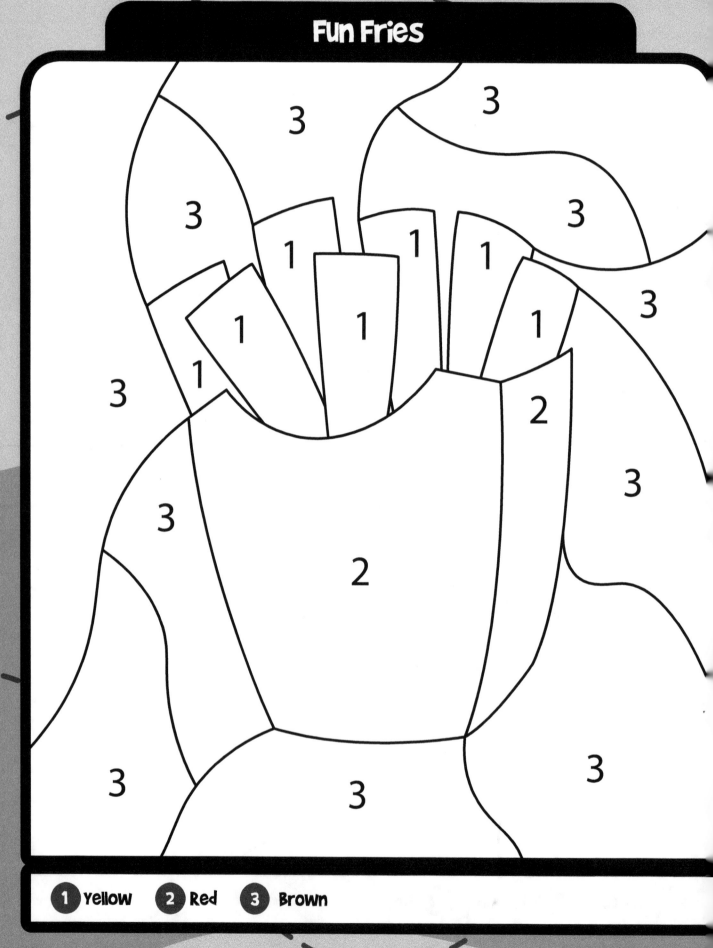

Hefty Hamburger

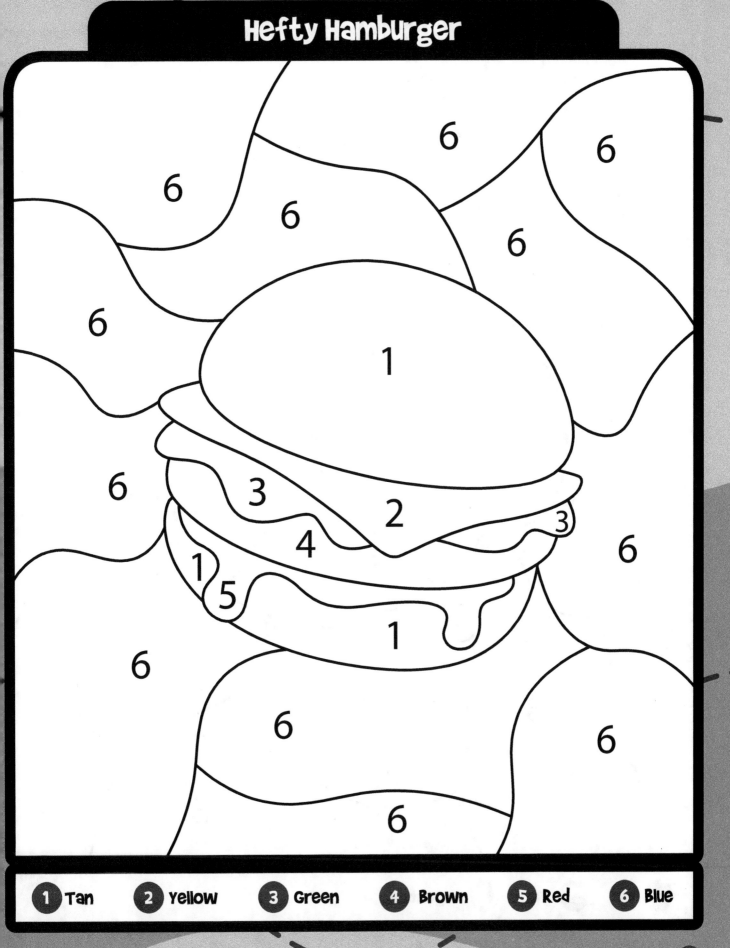

1 Tan   2 Yellow   3 Green   4 Brown   5 Red   6 Blue

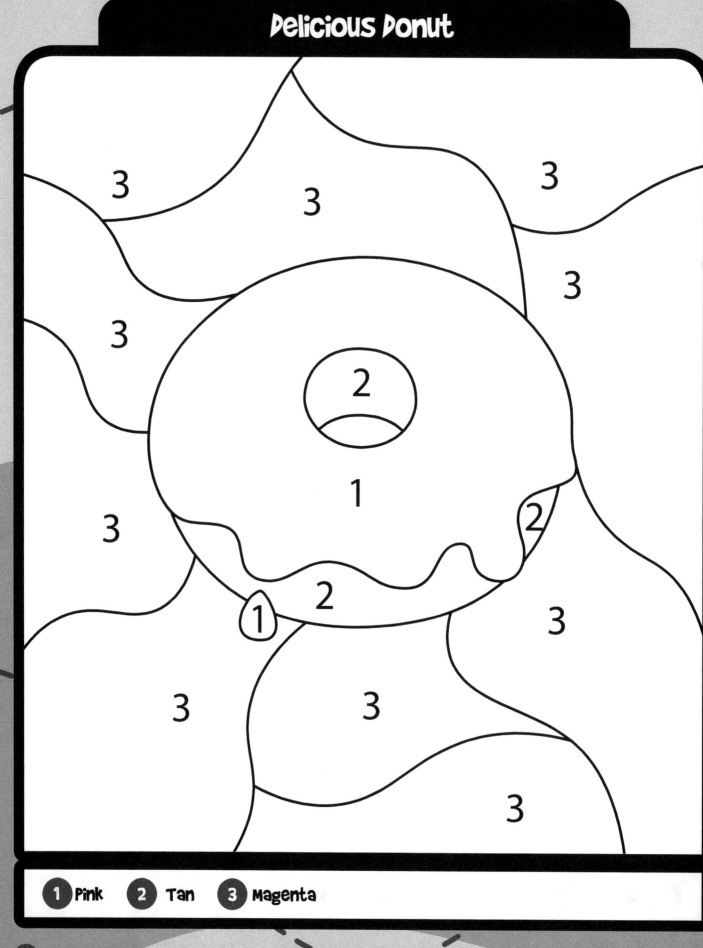

1 Pink   2 Tan   3 Magenta

Perfect Pizza

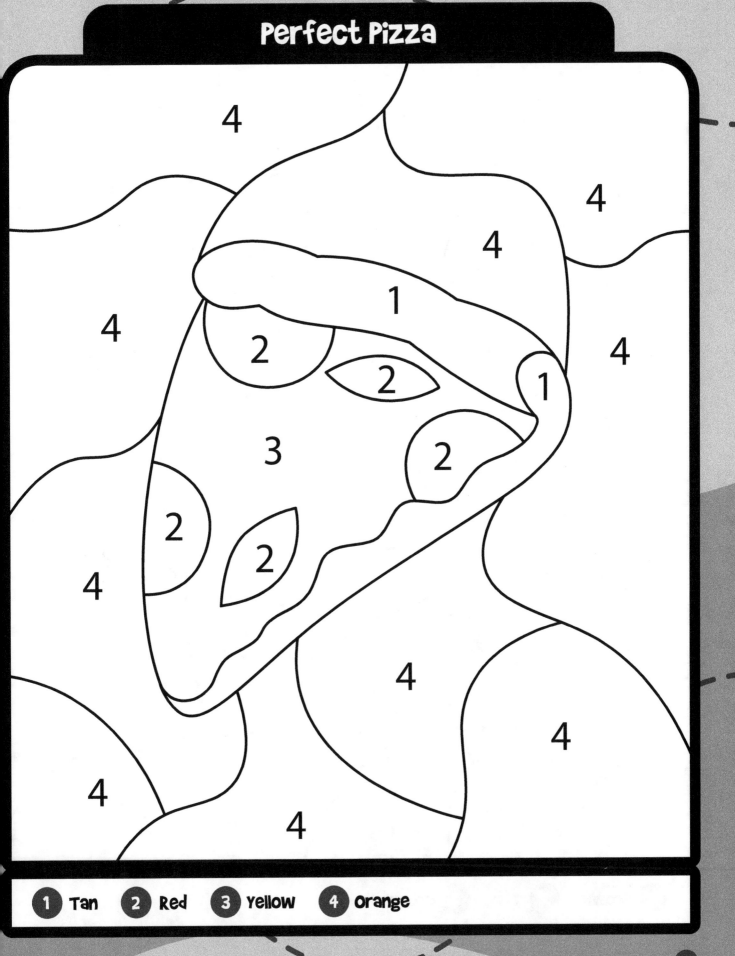

1 Tan   2 Red   3 Yellow   4 Orange

Terrific Treat

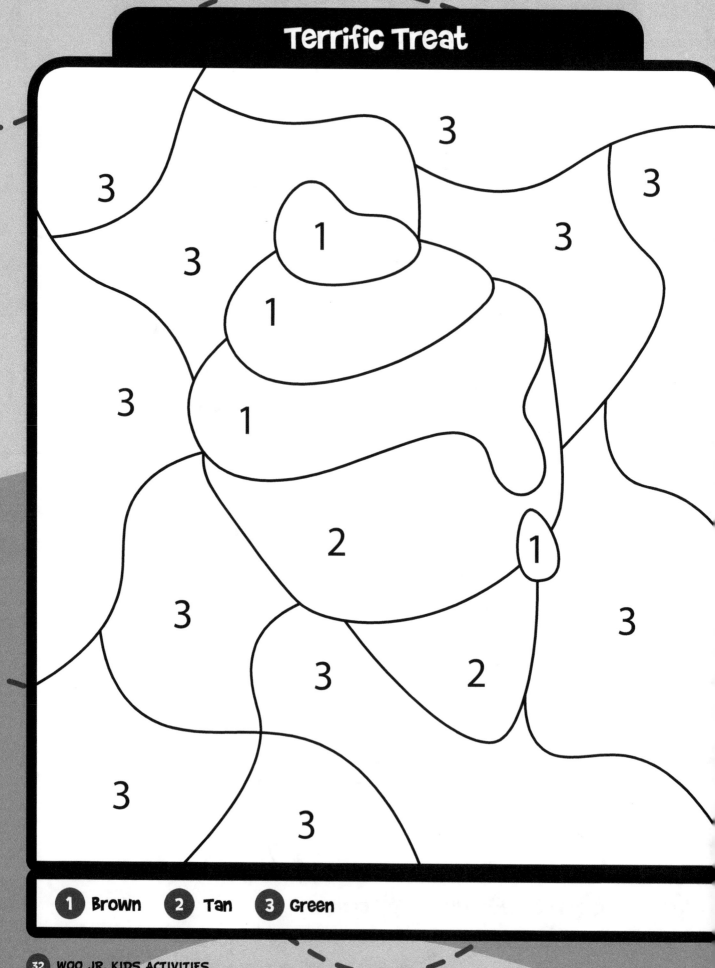

1 Brown 2 Tan 3 Green

Striking Storm

Radiant Rainbow

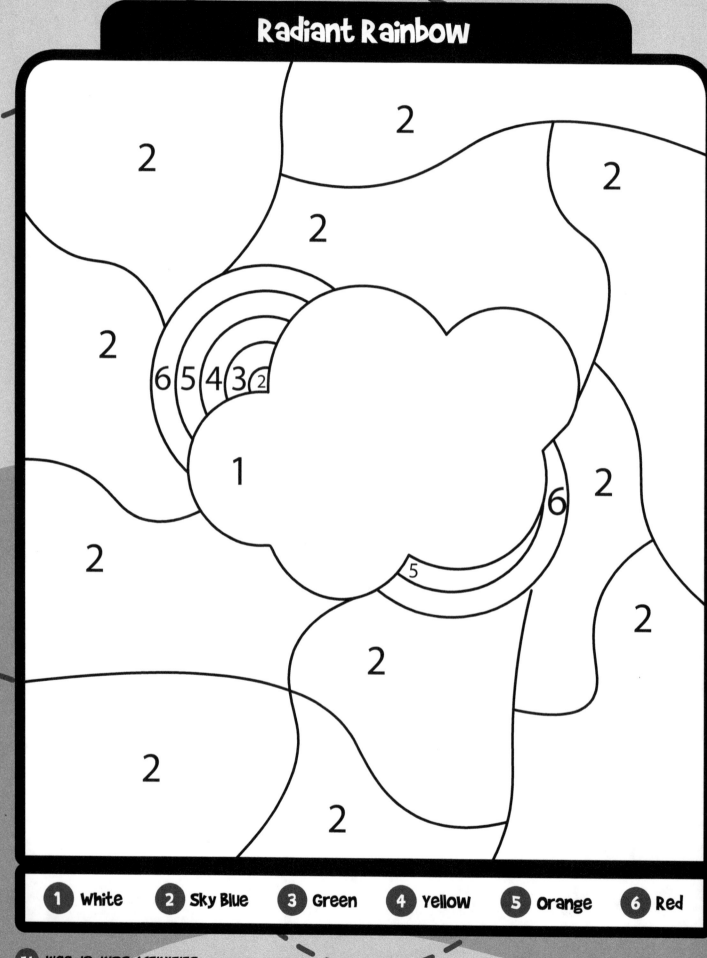

1 White   2 Sky Blue   3 Green   4 Yellow   5 Orange   6 Red

Shining Sun

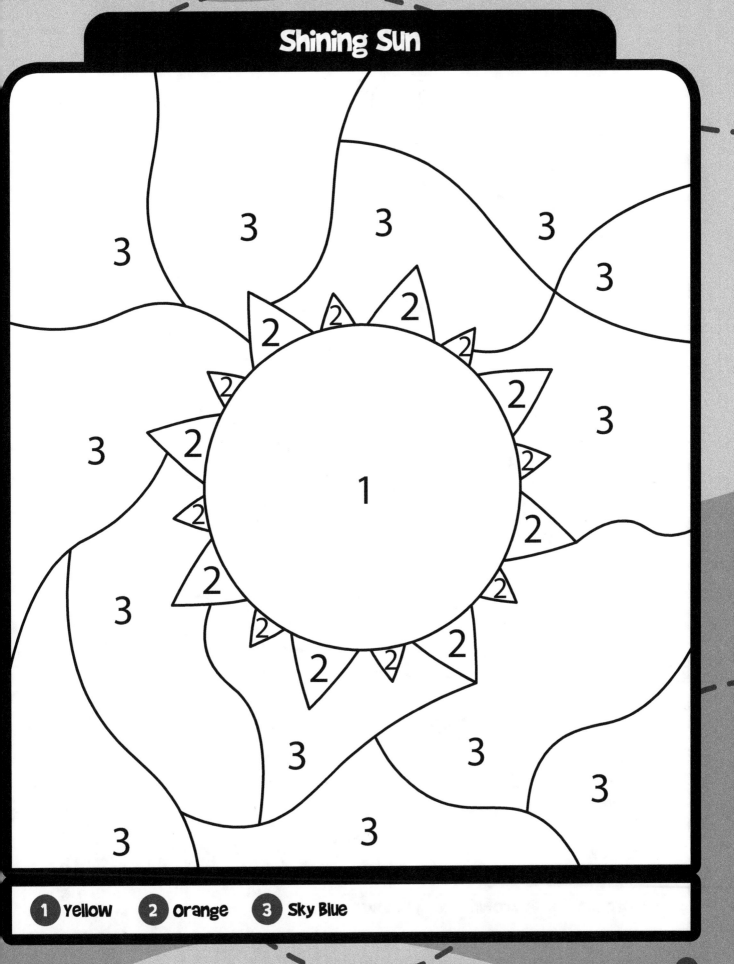

1 Yellow **2** Orange **3** Sky Blue

Pudgy Pumpkin

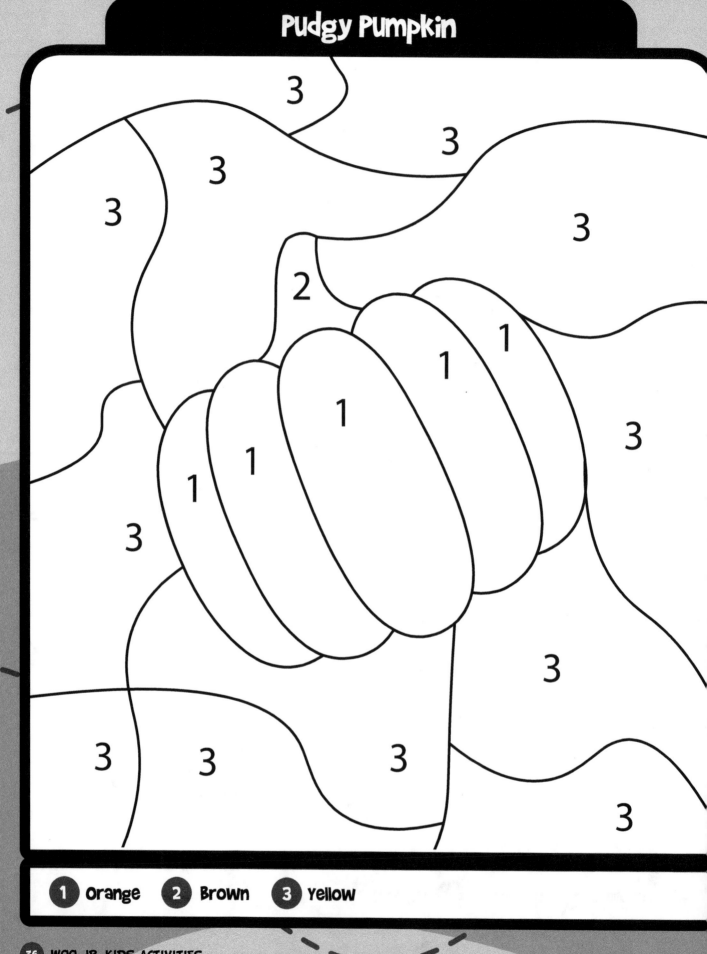

1 Orange   2 Brown   3 Yellow

Starry Satellite

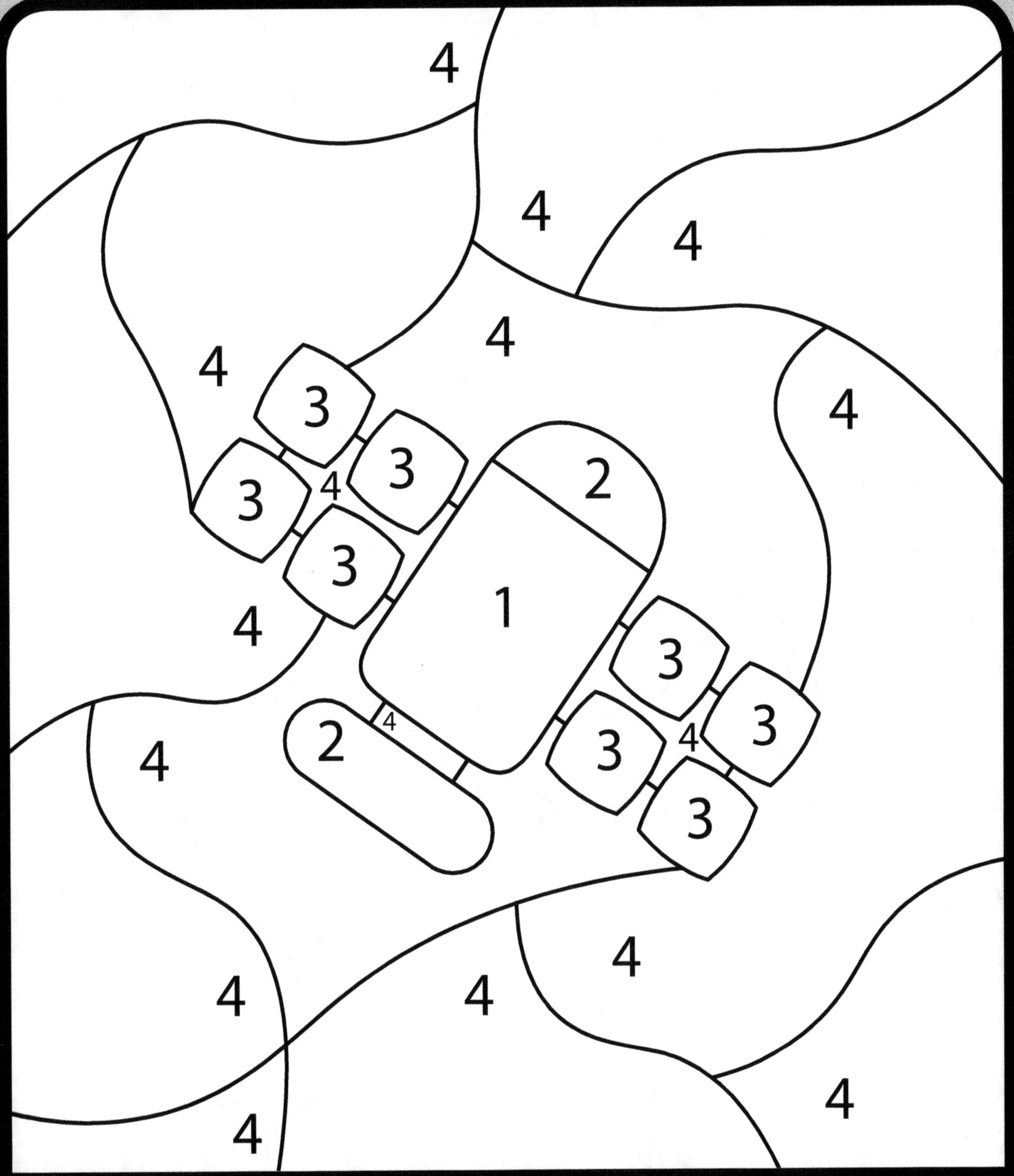

4

4

4

4

4

4

4

3

3

3

4 3

2

3

1

4

3

3

2 4

3

4 3

3

4

4

4

4

4

4

4

1 Black   2 Yellow   3 Gray   4 Blue

Ready Rocket

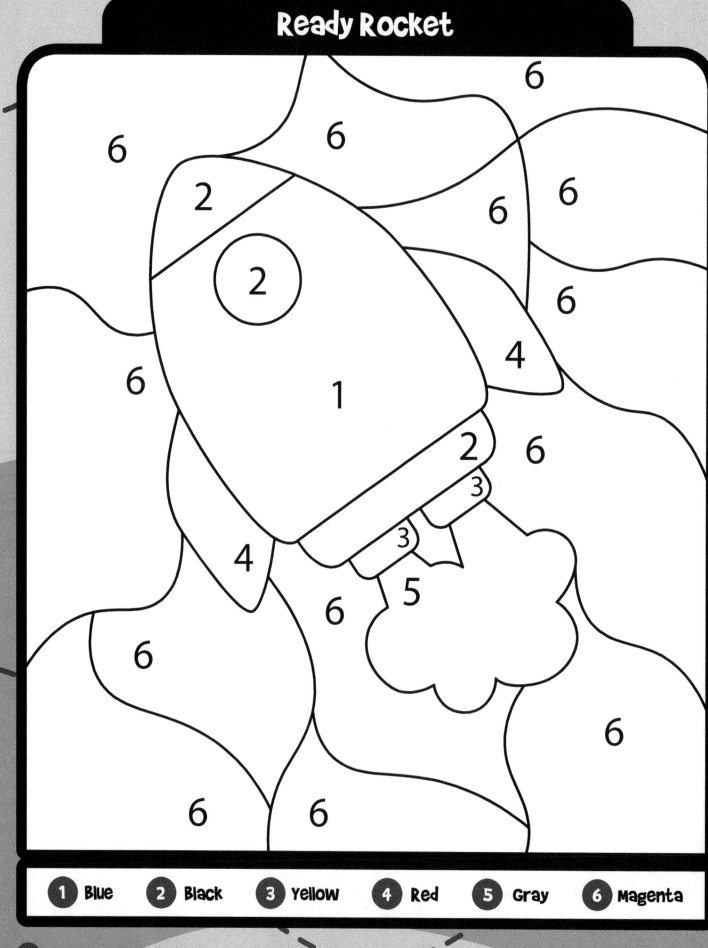

Popular Planet

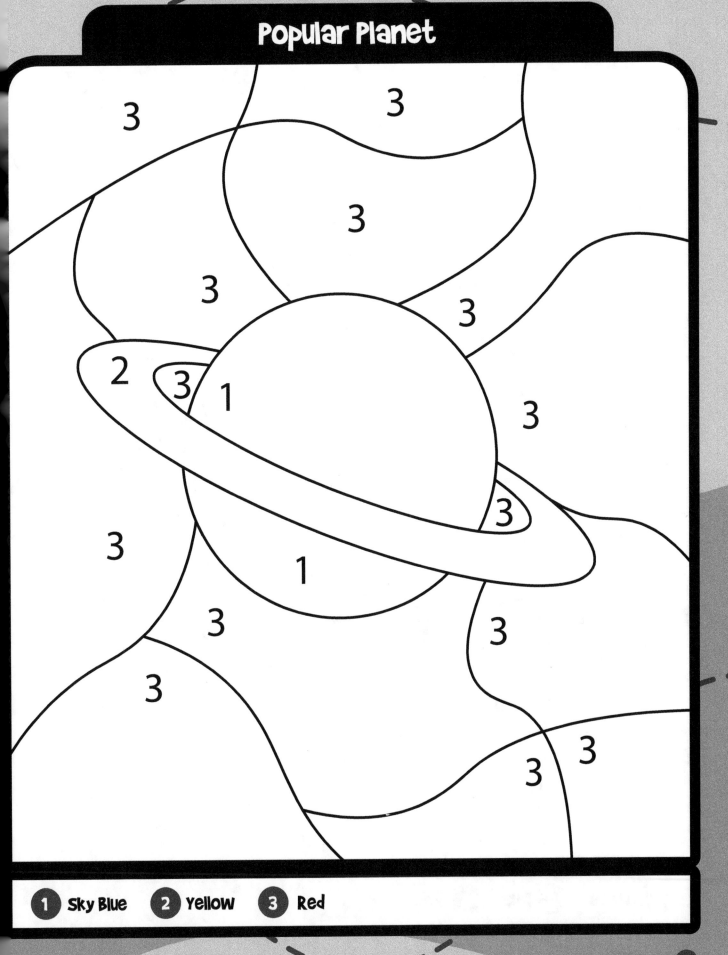

1 Sky Blue 2 Yellow 3 Red

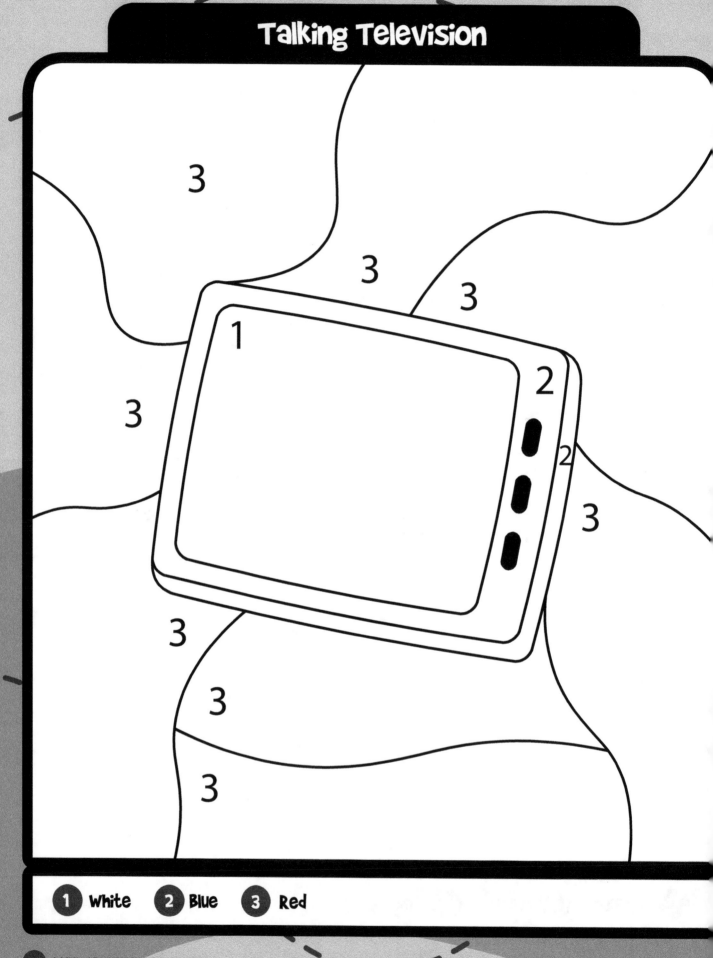

1 White **2** Blue **3** Red

Ghoulish Ghost

3 3 3 3 3

3

3

3 2 1 3

3

3 3

3 3 3 3

3

1 Pink   **2** Orange   **3** Sky Blue

Ferocious Fiend

3 3 3 3 3
2
3
3
2
1
3
3
2
3
3
3
3
3

① Hot Pink ② Brown ③ Pink

Beastly Blob

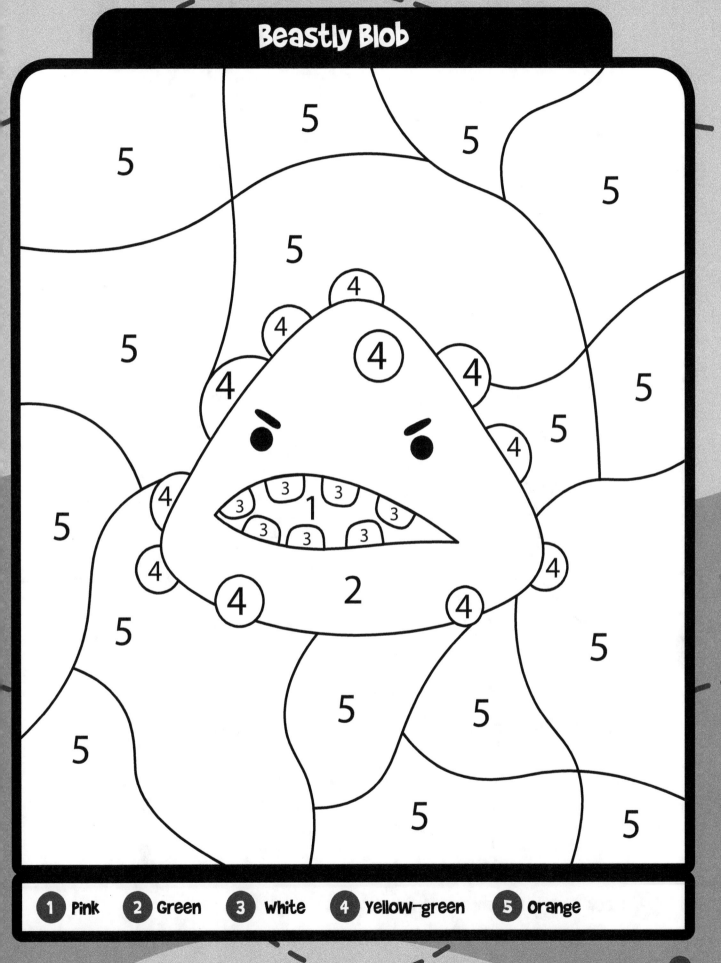

Greedy Goblin

1 Black **2** Magenta **3** Yellow

Deceitful Devil

1 White   2 Pink   3 Red   4 Yellow-green

Spooky Specter

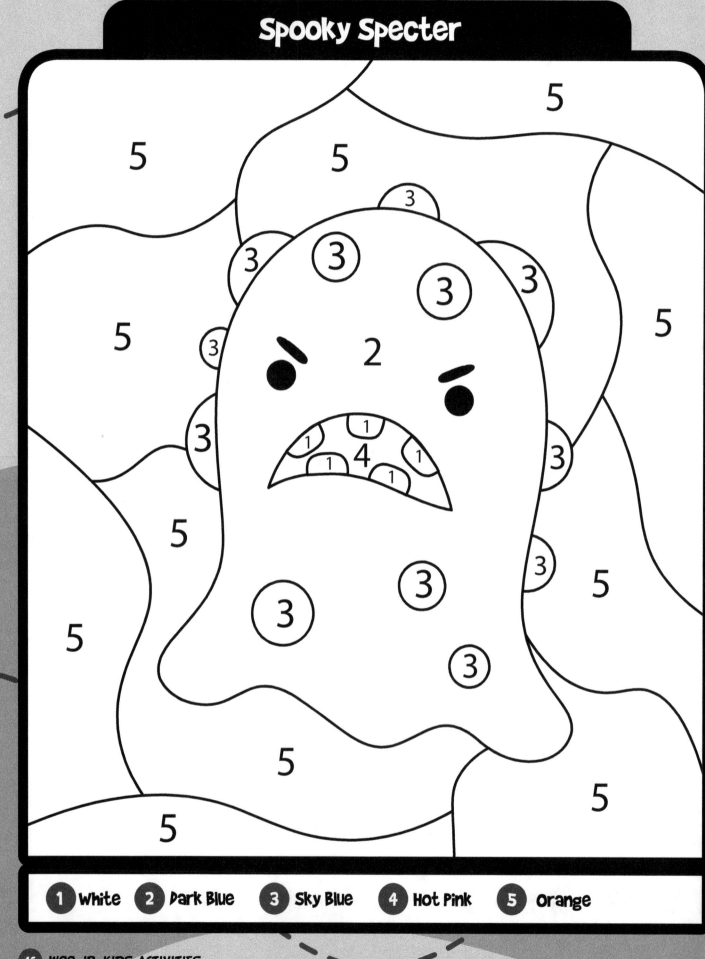

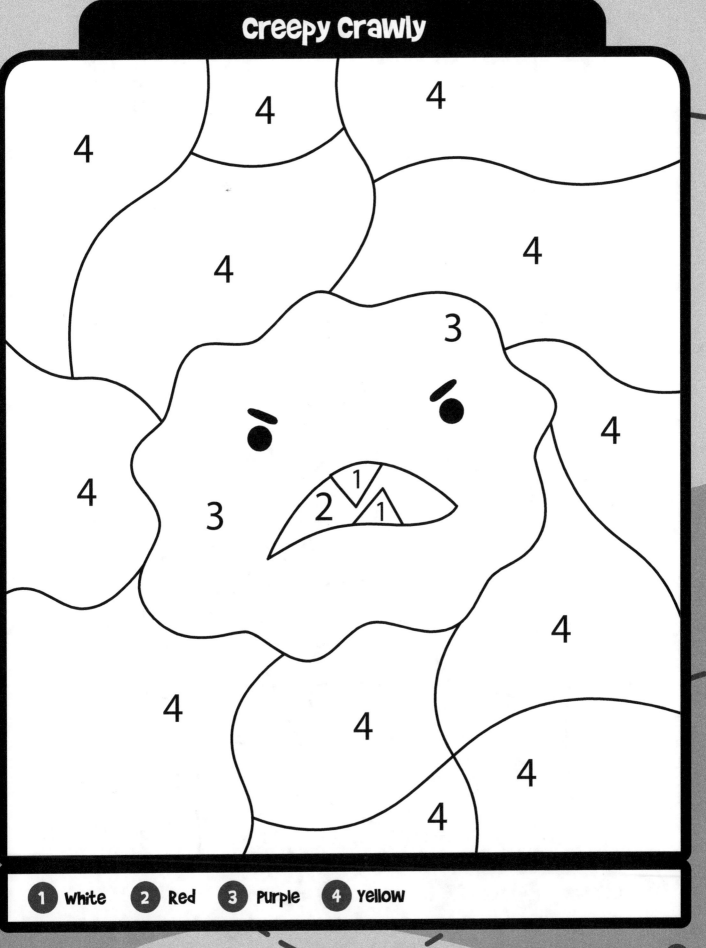

1 White   2 Red   3 Purple   4 Yellow

Menacing Monster

1 Hot Pink   **2** Yellow   **3** Purple

Shiny Shell

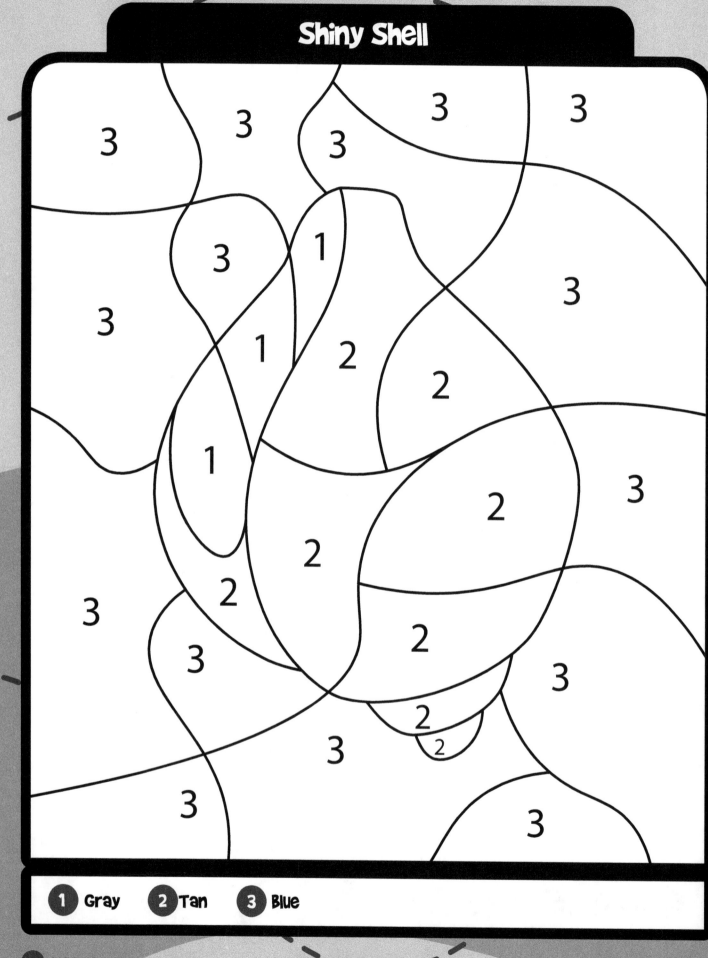

1 Gray   **2** Tan   **3** Blue

Tropical Tree

Seaworthy Starfish

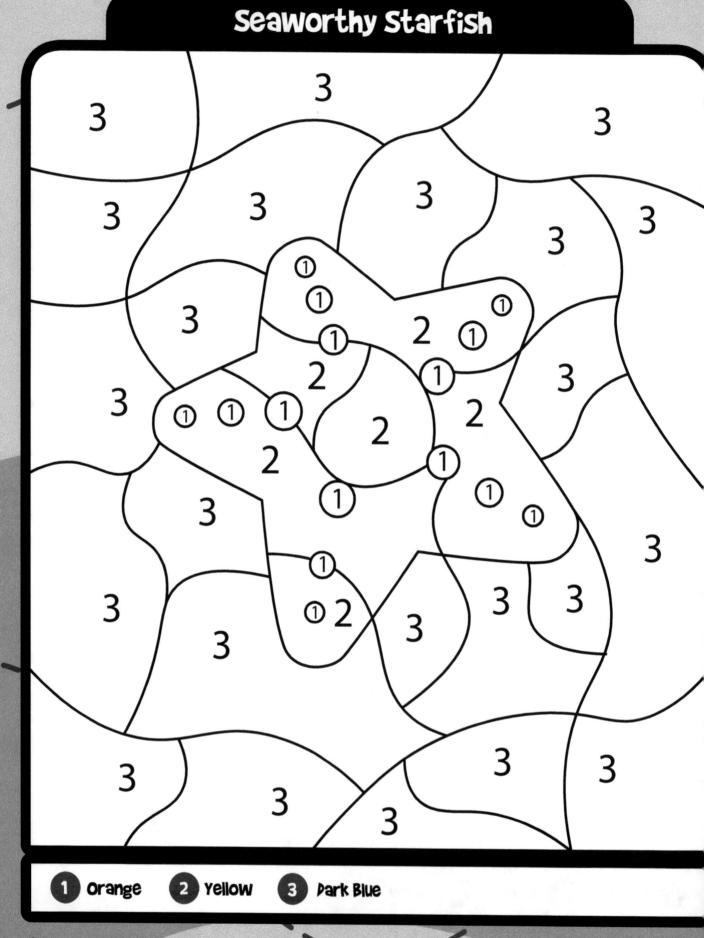

Beaming Beach Ball

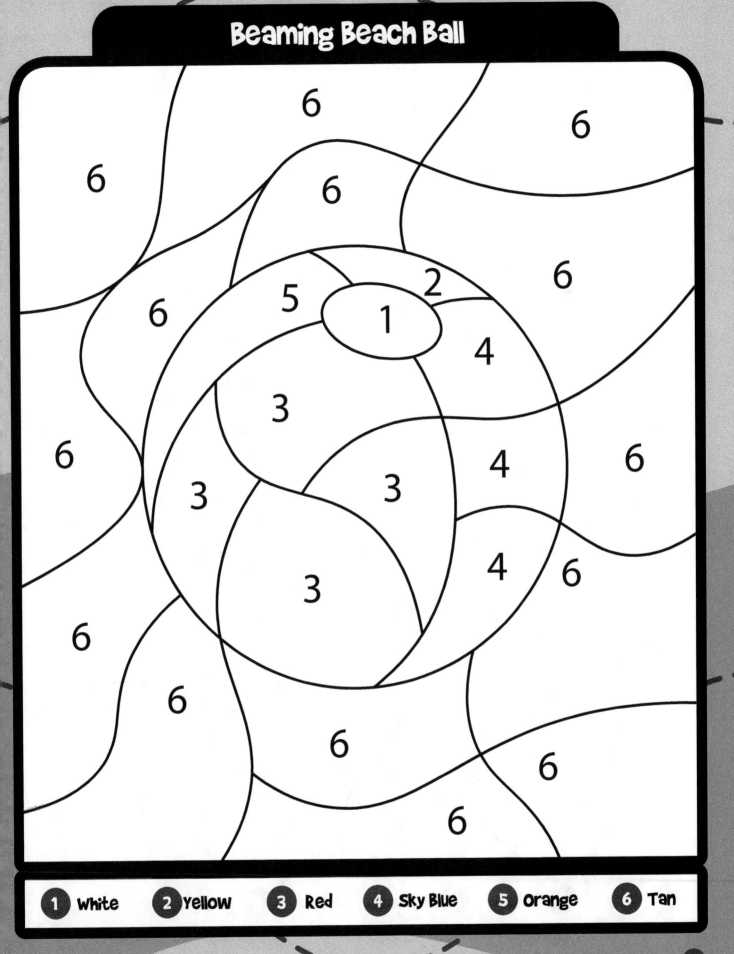

Pleasing Parasol

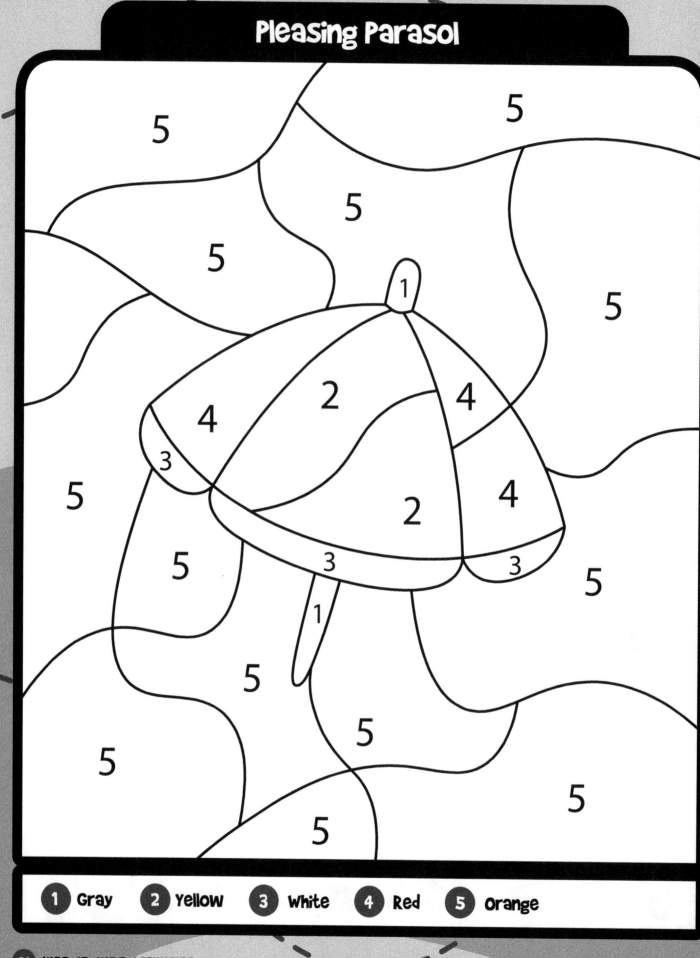

Wonderful Watermelon

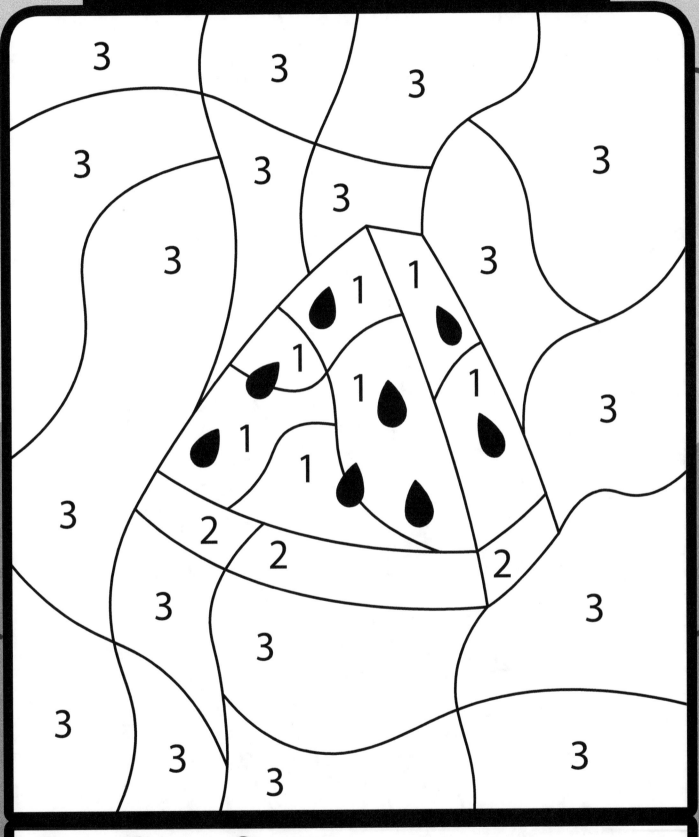

1 Red 2 Green 3 Purple

Bursting Blossom

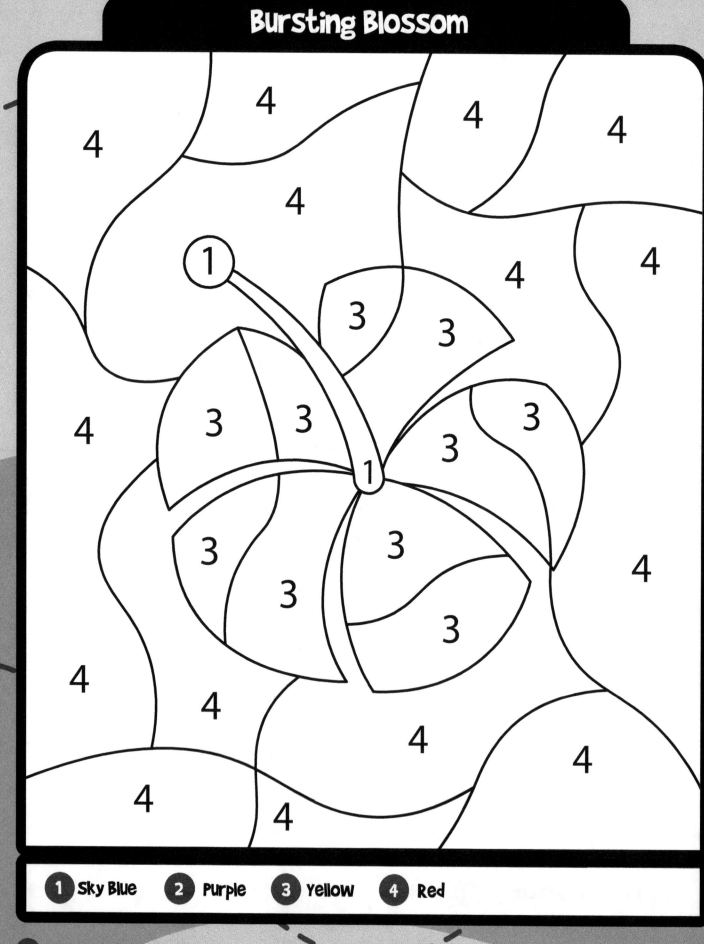

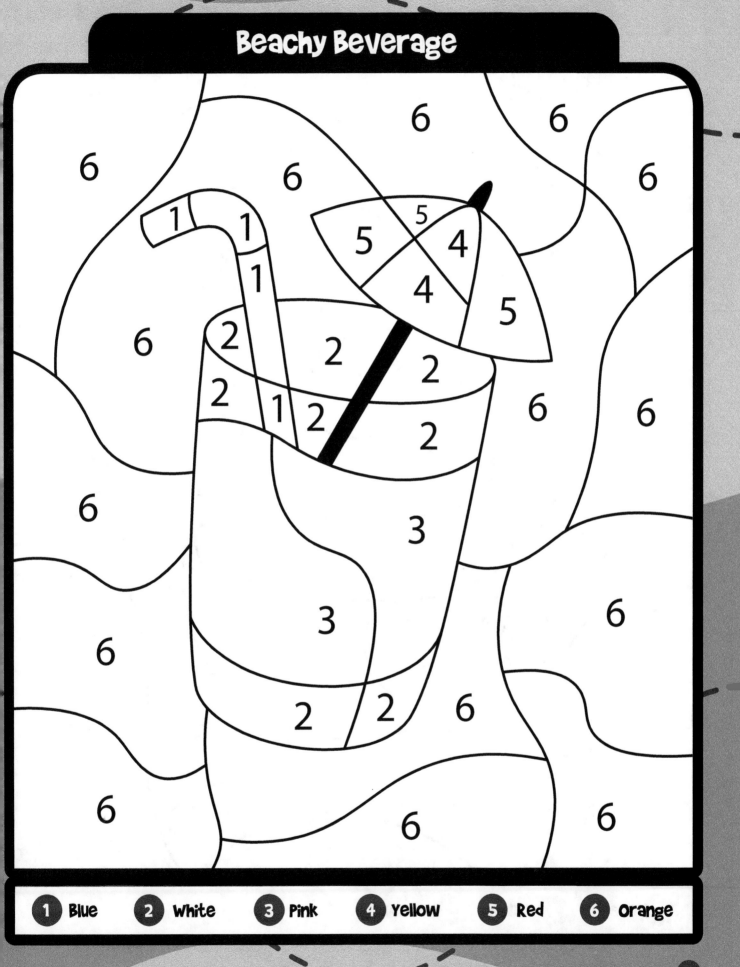

Plump Pineapple

1 Green **2** Yellow **3** Brown

Flourishing Flower

5   5   5

5

5

5

5   5   5

5   4   3   4   3
3   3   3   3
4   2   2   4
3   3   2   1   2   3   3
1
4   3   2   2   3   4
3   3   3
4   4
3   3
4   3   4
3

5   5

5

5   5

5   5

5   5

Shimmering Star

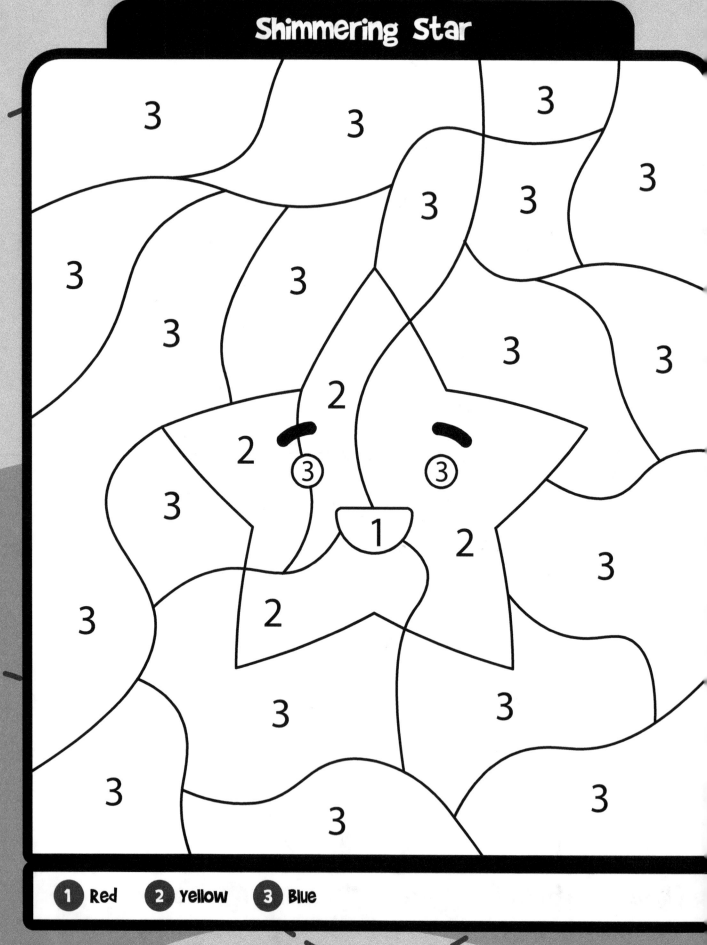

1 Red 2 Yellow 3 Blue

Silly Salamander

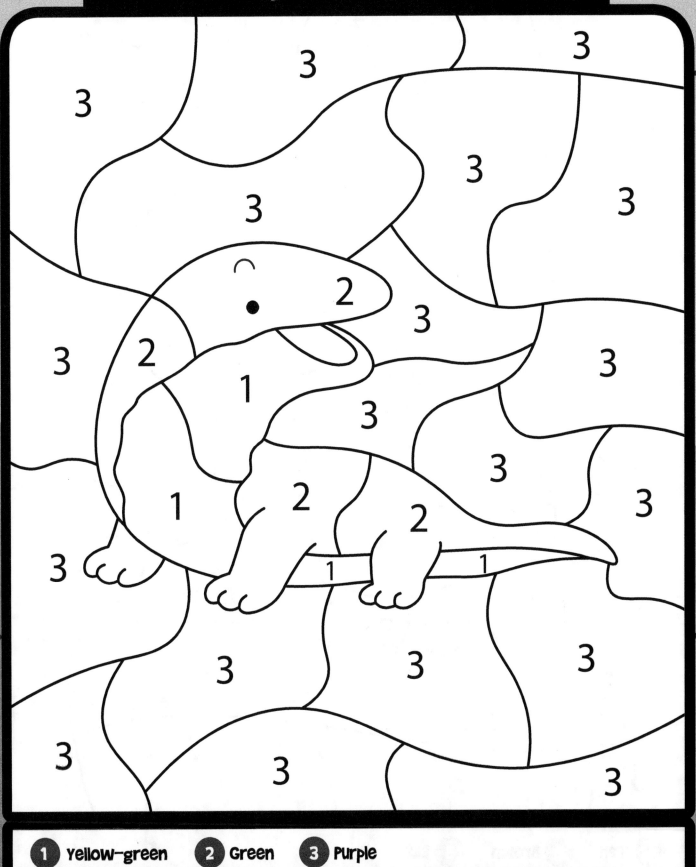

careful camel

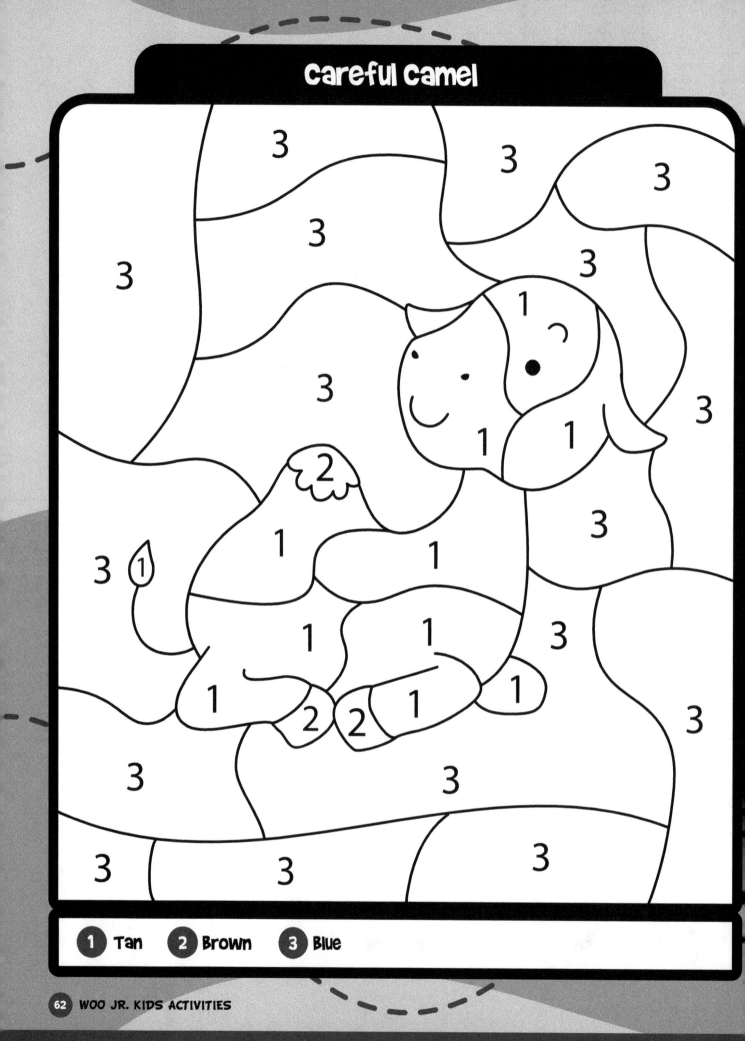

Mindful Meerkat

1 Brown   2 Tan   3 Green

Determined Donkey

Prickly Pincushion

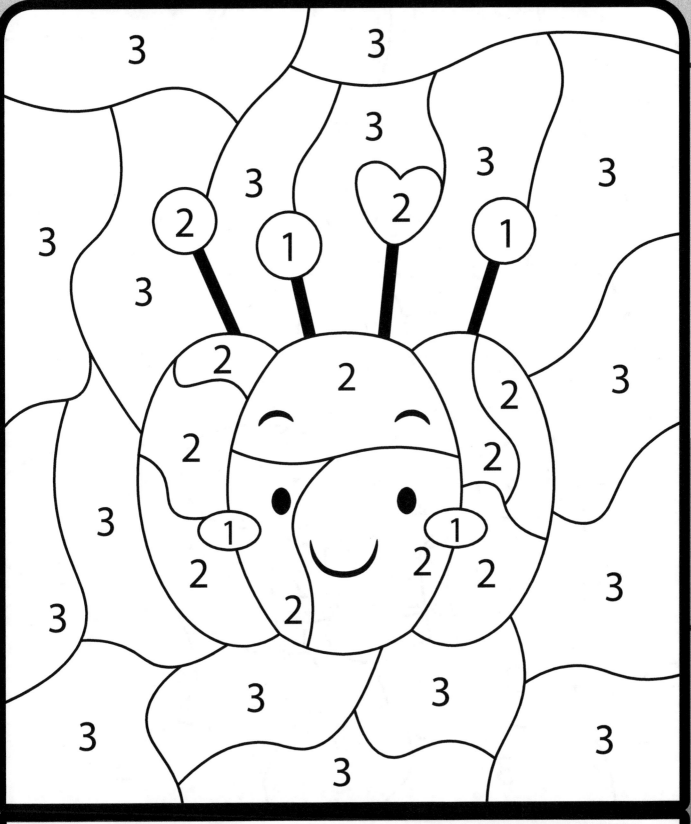

1 Pink 2 Red 3 Green

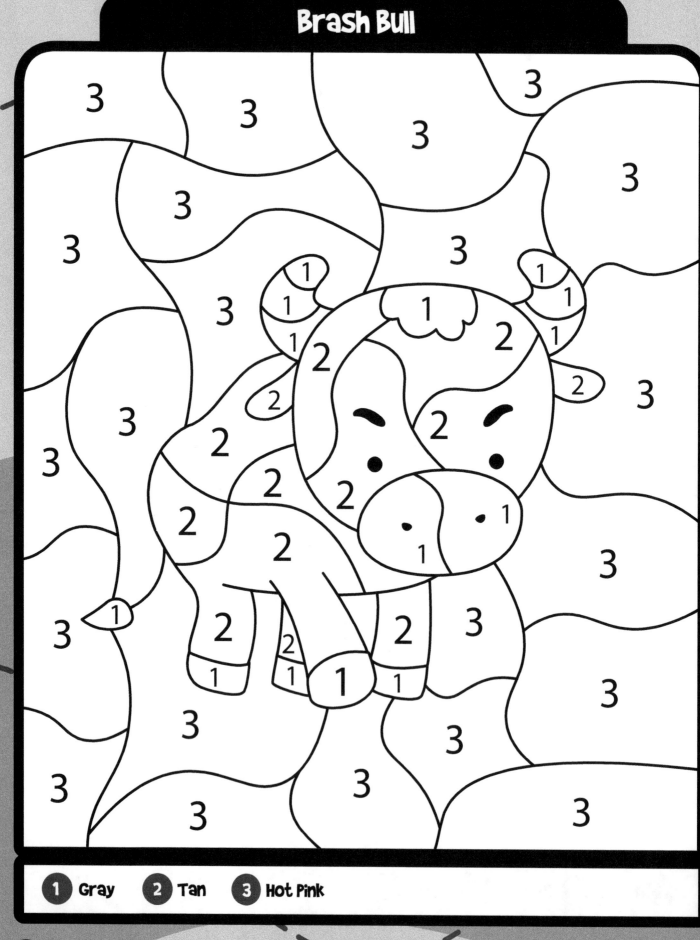

1 Gray   **2** Tan   **3** Hot Pink

Clucking Chicken

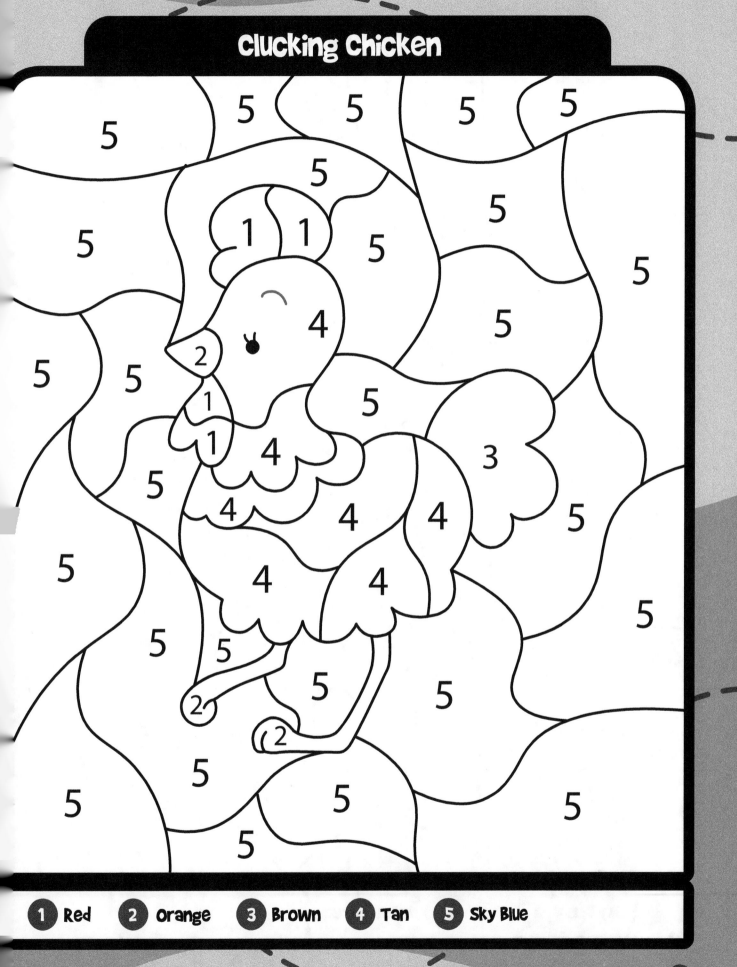

1 Red 2 Orange 3 Brown 4 Tan 5 Sky Blue

Precious Puppy

1 Sky Blue   **2** Blue   **3** Yellow-green

Lively Lemur

1 Tan   2 Brown   3 Pink

Fanciful Fish

1 Red   2 Dark Blue   3 Red   4 Tan   5 Yellow-green

capable crab

4   4   4   4

4   4   4

4   4

4   4   4

4   4   4   4

4   4   5   4   5   1   1   4

1   4   1   1   4   4

1   1   2   2   2   4

2   2   3   2   2

4   2   4

4   4   4

4   4   4

4   4   4

4   4   4

1 Red   **2** Tan   **3** Pink   **4** Blue   **5** White

Slimy Snail

1 Purple 2 Magenta 3 Pink 4 Yellow 5 White

Thrilling Thread

1 Gray   2 Hot Pink   3 Black   4 Pink   5 Magenta

Mischievous Monkey

1 Tan   2 Pink   3 Brown   4 Green

1 Yellow-green   2 White   3 Brown   4 Orange   5 Pink   6 Blue

Leaping Llama

1 Tan 2 Brown 3 Sky Blue

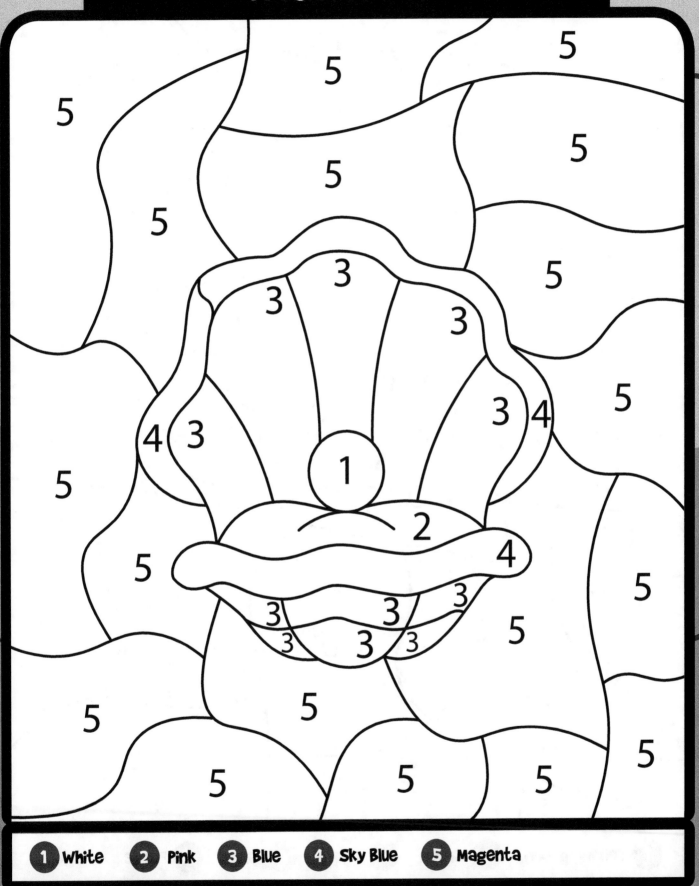

1 White   2 Pink   3 Blue   4 Sky Blue   5 Magenta

1 Yellow-green   2 Green   3 White   4 Gray   5 Purple

1 Tan 2 Black 3 Brown 4 Yellow 5 Hot Pink 6 Pink

Beautiful Bird

1 Tan   2 Pink   3 Brown   4 Dark Blue

Wiggly Worm

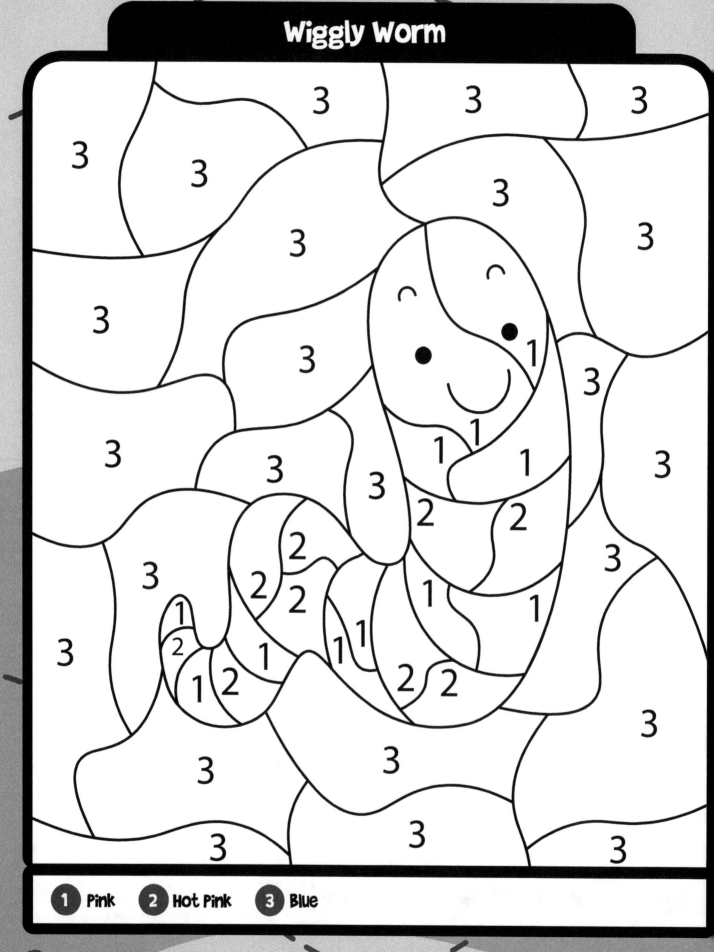

1 Pink   2 Hot Pink   3 Blue

Plucky Penguin

Slithering Snake

1 Yellow   2 Hot Pink

1 Blue 2 Sky Blue 3 White 4 Yellow

Gentle Giraffe

1 Yellow   2 Brown   3 Tan

Elegant Elephant

Wild Whale

Opulent Ostrich

1 Gray   2 Black   3 Pink   4 Sky Blue

Grinning Gecko

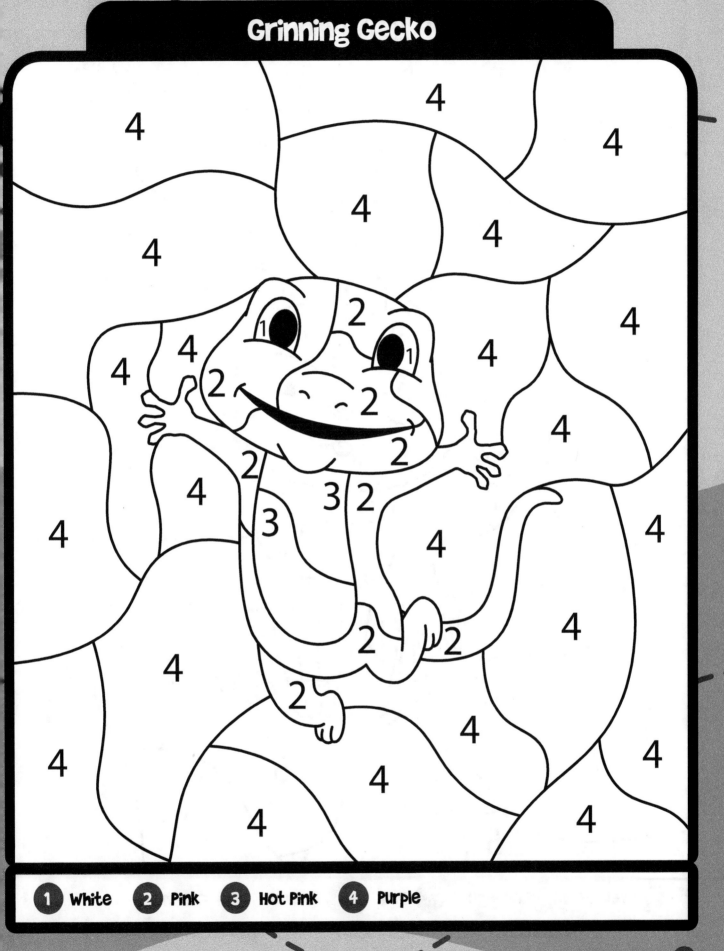

1 White   2 Pink   3 Hot Pink   4 Purple

Laughing Lion

1 Yellow 2 Orange 3 Pink 4 Brown 5 Green

Amiable Alligator

1 Green   **2** Yellow-green   **3** Purple

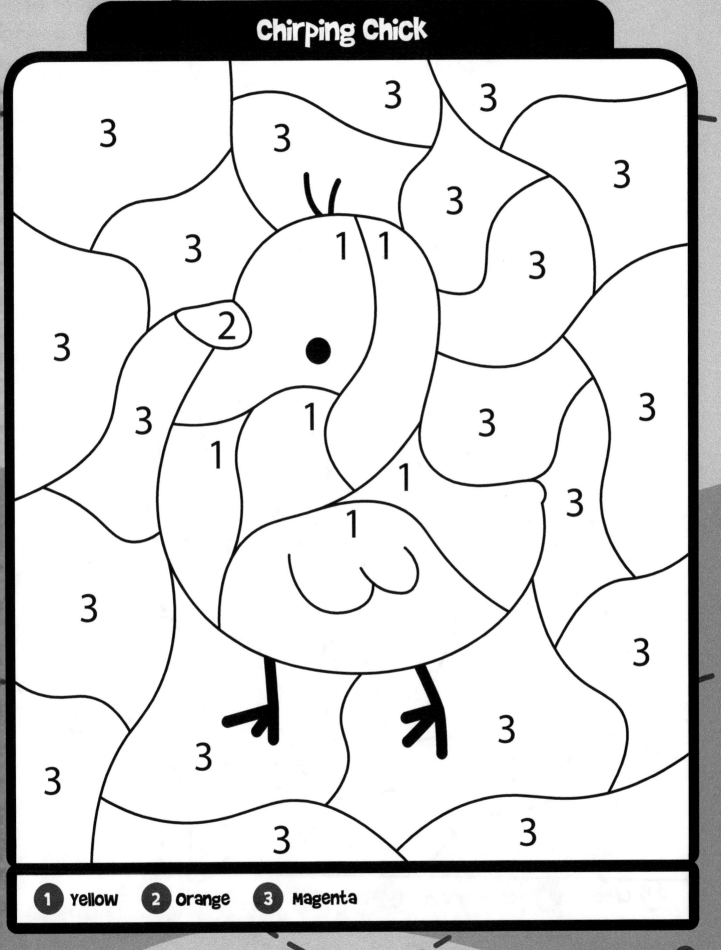

1 Yellow 2 Orange 3 Magenta

Tall T-Rex

1 Green   **2** Yellow-green   **3** Red   **4** Tan

Tricky Triceratops

Amazing Apatosaurus

3
3
3
3
3
3
1
3
1
3
3
3
1
1
1
2
3
1
3
1
3
2
3
1
3
1
1
3
3
3
3
3
3

1 Green   **2** Yellow-green   **3** Pink

Tremendous Pteranodon

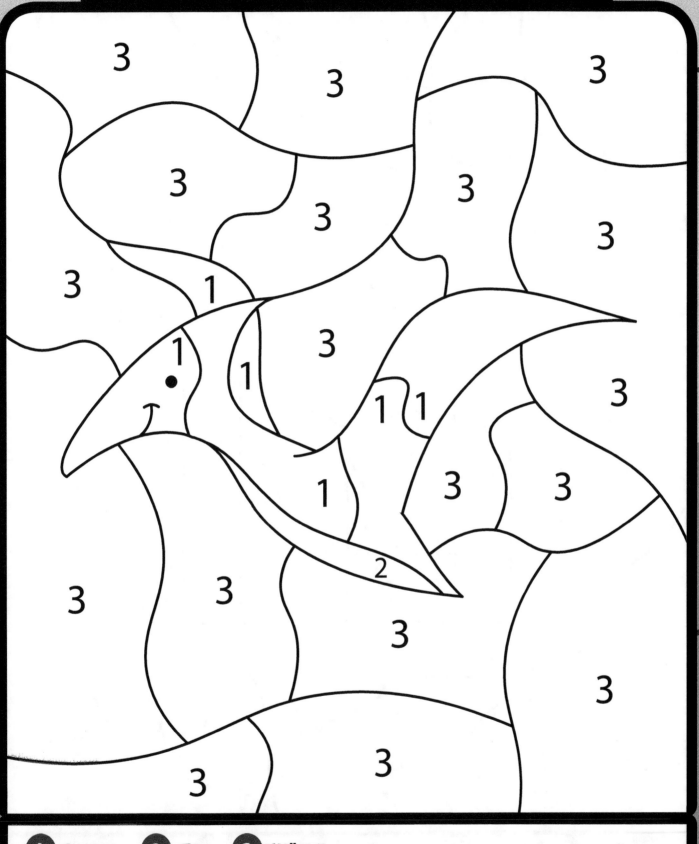

1 orange   **2** Tan   **3** Yellow

Blissful Barn

1 Red 2 Brown 3 Gray 4 Yellow-green 5 Sky Blue

Silly Circus Tent

1 Red   2 White   3 Black   4 Blue   5 Tan

cozy cabin

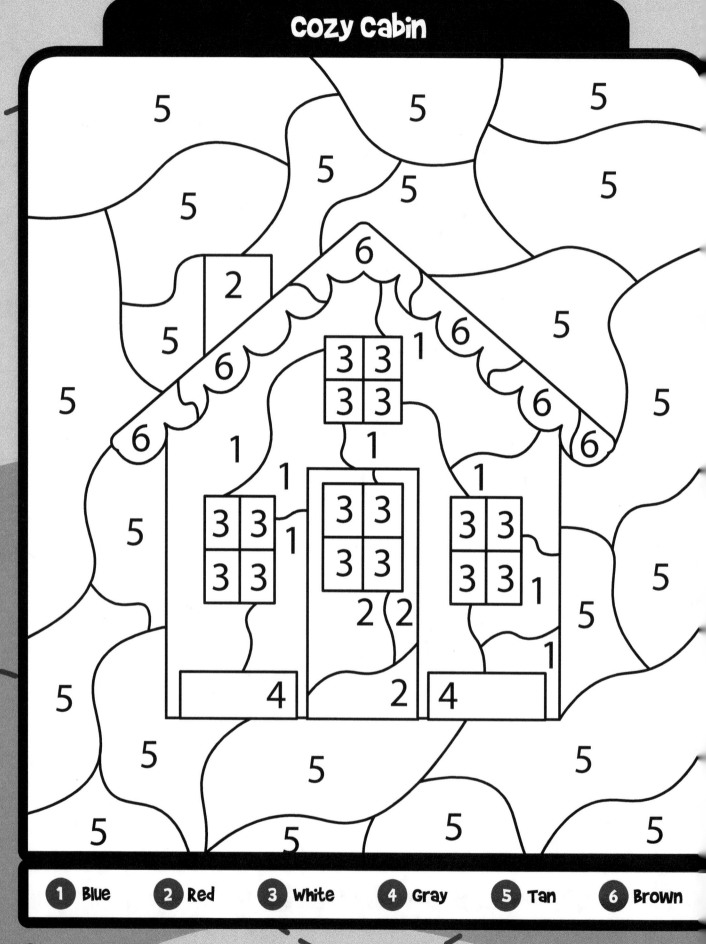

1 Blue   2 Red   3 White   4 Gray   5 Tan   6 Brown

Happy Home

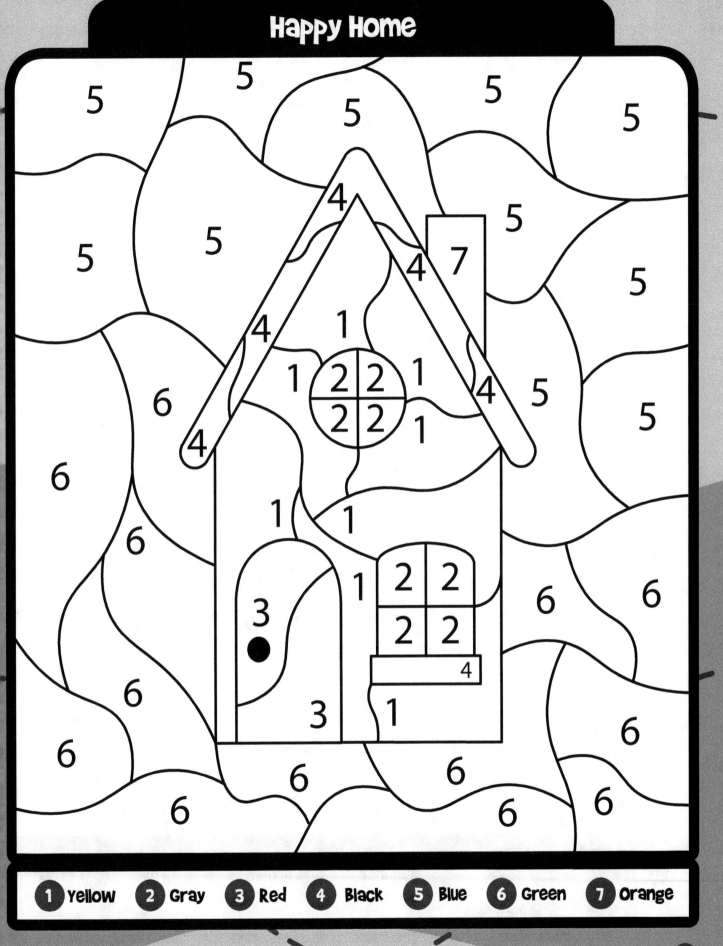

Pillaging Pirate

Hearty Hat

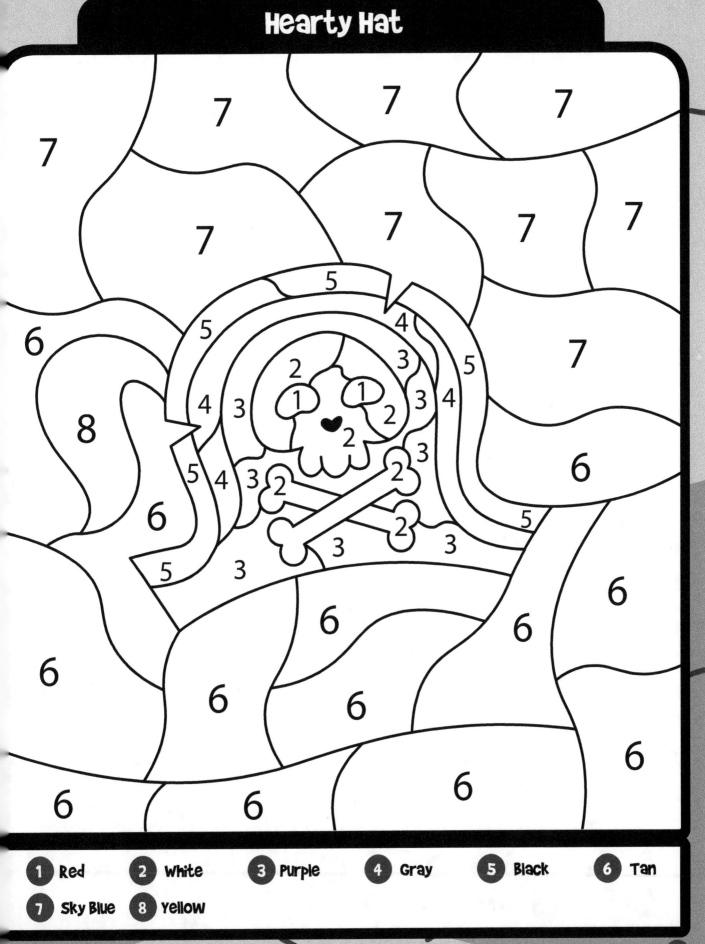

1. Red
2. White
3. Purple
4. Gray
5. Black
6. Tan
7. Sky Blue
8. Yellow

Helpful Hummingbird

1 Orange 2 Sky Blue 3 Dark Blue 4 Yellow 5 Green 6 Yellow-green

7 Pink 8 Hot Pink 9 Magenta

Adorable Animals!

7 7 7 7 7 7

7 7

7 7 7

7

7 7

7

5

5 1
1
5
5
8 8
5
5

9 6
6
6
9

10
10 10
6
9
8 9
8
8

5
5 5
6

10 10
3 1
1
4 7 2 1
9 1 8 1 1 3
4 8 8 5 6 5 8
8 8 8 8 8 8

4 4 4

4

4 4 4 4

4 4 4

4 4 4

| 1 | Orange | 2 | Dark Blue | 3 | Yellow | 4 | Yellow-green | 5 | Sky Blue | 6 | Gray |
| 7 | Blue | 8 | White | 9 | Tan | 10 | Brown |

DragonFruit, an imprint of Mango Publishing, publishes high-quality children's books to inspire a love of lifelong learning in readers. DragonFruit publishes a variety of titles for kids, including children's picture books, nonfiction series, toddler activity books, pre-K activity books, science and education titles, and ABC books. Beautiful and engaging, our books celebrate diversity, spark curiosity, and capture the imaginations of parents and children alike.

Mango Publishing, established in 2014, publishes an eclectic list of books by diverse authors. We were named the Fastest-Growing Independent Publisher by Publishers Weekly in 2019 and 2020. Our success is bolstered by our main goal, which is to publish high-quality books that will make a positive impact in people's lives.

Our readers are our most important resource; we value your input, suggestions, and ideas. We'd love to hear from you—after all, we are publishing books for you!

Please stay in touch with us and follow us at:

Instagram: @dragonfruitkids

Facebook: Mango Publishing

Twitter: @MangoPublishing

LinkedIn: Mango Publishing

Pinterest: Mango Publishing

Sign up for our newsletter at www.mangopublishinggroup.com and receive a free book! Join us on Mango's journey to change publishing, one book at a time.

Woo! Jr. Kids Activities is passionate about inspiring children to learn through imagination and FUN. That is why we have provided thousands of craft ideas, printables, and teacher resources to over 55 million people since 2008. We are on a mission to produce books that allow kids to build knowledge, express their talent, and grow into creative, compassionate human beings. Elementary education teachers, day care professionals, and parents have come to rely on Woo! Jr. for high-quality, engaging, and innovative content that children LOVE. Our bestselling kids activity books have sold over 375,000 copies worldwide.

Tap into our free kids activity ideas at our website WooJr.com or by following us on social media: